The 90-Minute Resume

The 90-Minute Resume

Second Edition

Peggy Schmidt

Peterson's Guides
Princeton, New Jersey

Library of Congress Cataloging-in-Publication Data
Schmidt, Peggy J.
        The 90-minute resume / Peggy Schmidt. — 2nd ed.
            p.   cm.
        ISBN 1-56079-150-0
        1. Resumes (Employment). 2. Applications for positions.
    I. Title. II. Title: Ninety-minute resume.
    HF5383.S325   1992
    650.14—dc20   92-6958

Composition and design by Peterson's Guides

Printed in the United States of America

10 9 8 7 6 5 4 3 2 1

Contents

Acknowledgments

My deepest thanks to those who have contributed their ideas to the revision of *The 90-Minute Resume.*

Lynn Tendler Bignell, principal and cofounder, Gilbert Tweed Associates, New York, New York

Richard J. Chagnon, senior vice president/professional services, Right Associates, Philadelphia, Pennsylvania

Bill Davis, director of marketing, Minotype Typography, Chicago, Illinois.

John D. Erdlen, president, Management Dimensions, Inc., and director, Northeast Human Resources Association, Wellesley, Massachusetts

Susan Gordon, president, Lynne Palmer Agency, New York, New York

Virginia Lord, senior vice president/marketing and public relations, Right Associates, Philadelphia, Pennsylvania

Jeanne Miller, public relations coordinator, AlphaGraphics, Tucson, Arizona

Jack Schwartz, area managing director, Source Edp, New York, New York

Barbara Stafford, manager of electronic graphics, AlphaGraphics commercial printing division, Tucson, Arizona

My editors, Jim Gish, Owen O'Donnell, Joy Mastroberardino, and the Peterson's staff

Many thanks to my family—Joe, Ted, and Christina—for their support.

Preface

After my book *Making It on Your First Job: When You're Young, Ambitious, and Inexperienced* came out, relatives and friends—and friends of friends—began asking me to help them put together or revise their resume. The approach I used and refined over time was based on my years of experience and training as a journalist: I asked the job hunter questions in the same way I would if I'd been interviewing him or her for an article. The technique seemed to work no matter who I was helping—my brother, a recent college graduate; a friend who had worked in one profession for ten years but wanted to change careers; my mother, who was going back to work after a twenty-five-year hiatus. "You made me look great!" they told me. They got interviews and they landed good jobs.

I began passing along the highlights of my interview technique to students at the New York University Summer Publishing Institute, where I'm the career coordinator. I've reviewed hundreds of resumes since 1982 and have seen dramatic improvements after students followed my suggestions. Many have told me that they felt much more confident about starting their job search because they knew their resume portrayed them at their best.

I decided to self-publish my "interview approach" to resume writing and offer it to readers of the weekly column I was writing for New York's *Daily News*. Hundreds wrote in to ask for a copy, and some of those called back to say that after following the guide they'd received compliments on their resume from the employers they'd interviewed with.

That prompted me to restudy the resume books on my bookshelf and the latest releases in bookstores. I found they were thick with sample resumes and jammed with self-assessment exercises, but short on the kind of advice that I considered really helpful. Maybe, I told myself, more people than I'd originally thought could benefit from *The 90-Minute Resume.*

I expanded and revised the original guide, incorporating the suggestions of readers who had used it. The first edition was published by Peterson's in the spring of 1990.

I owe many thanks to the readers of the first edition who helped make its publication a success. Because I want to offer even more help to job hunters, I have expanded and revised the book. I regularly interview employers for my syndicated newspaper column, "Your New Job," and continue to pick up the latest thinking of those who evaluate resumes. In this revised edition, there are new sections that allow you to test your resume expertise, present resume makeovers, and offer suggestions about how to get your resume into the hands of decision makers.

There's no tougher assignment than sitting down in front of a blank piece of paper and trying to figure out what to say about yourself. But if you ask someone to act as an interviewer and talk you through the process, you can create a strong marketing piece that can help you land a great job.

I'm the kind of person who would like to play the role of interviewer with every job hunter who needs help with his or her resume. Since I can't do that, I'm honored that you've decided to have me as the unseen muse who, I hope, will inspire you and your coach to produce a truly outstanding resume.

Peggy Schmidt
April 1992

Introduction

In the course of my career, I've had the opportunity to compare thousands of resumes and have given suggestions to hundreds of job seekers about how to make theirs better. In the process, I learned five important things:

1. Candidates with similar credentials can come across as more or less qualified depending on what they say or don't say—and how well they say it.
2. It is possible to portray yourself as a terrific job candidate without misrepresenting the truth, even if you don't have much job experience, a top grade point average, or strong academic credentials.
3. You can communicate your experience effectively on paper even if writing is not your strongest skill.
4. The content and design of your resume can result in your being asked in for an interview—or being deep-sixed in a file cabinet.
5. A job hunter stands a better chance of getting hired if his or her resume is conceived with prospective employers' needs in mind.

Think of your resume as you would a coming attraction for a movie; if the preview is enticing, you're going to want to see the film when it is released. Similarly, a carefully conceived resume can result in a call for an interview. What makes for a winning resume? First, it must be visually inviting—clean and highly readable. Second, it should highlight your experiences and skills in an easy-to-follow format. Third, and perhaps most important, it should reflect the results of your experience, not simply provide job descriptions.

You can create a great resume in a relatively short period of time by using the method that I've developed from years of teaching resume-writing workshops and working with individuals to perfect their resumes. I've found it to be not only the quickest but also the best way to get experience and skills down on paper; it's called the interview method.

How does it work? Find a person, someone who is familiar with your background and who, preferably, already has had the experience of putting together a resume or is currently doing so, to play the role of **interviewer.** That person might be a friend, former colleague, classmate, parent, brother, or sister. The job of the interviewer (that's how he or she will be referred to throughout the book) is to ask you, the **job hunter** (that's how you'll be referred to), questions about your education, work experience, activities, skills, and interests.

This book contains all the information the two of you need to produce a resume that will portray you at your best. Before you schedule an interview time, be sure to skim through *The 90-Minute Resume* to get an idea of how it works. There are several things you'll want to prepare in advance; these are discussed in the section called "First, Your Fact Sheets," on page 19. It's also a good idea for the interviewer to familiarize himself or herself with the process. A quick read-through of the book is the best way, but if your interviewer doesn't have the time, have him or her read the entire "Preliminaries" section and the interviewer guidelines that are interspersed throughout the book.

Finally, keep this thought in mind as you work: Believe in yourself. Even if you think that you've done only ordinary things, you are a special person with unique experiences and skills. You *can* get a good first job.

The process of creating a resume is a very useful first step in your job search because it helps you focus your job objective and organize your experiences. Knowing where you're going and how your past experiences have prepared you to get there is essential for convincing an employer that you're the right candidate. Expressing your ambition and accomplishments on paper will give you confidence and direction as you begin your job search.

An hour and a half is a realistic time period in which to produce a solid draft of your resume (producing the final product is discussed in "Design Your Resume" on page 73 and is not included in the 90 minutes). Before you get together with your interviewer, you'll need to do some advance work to allow the process to proceed smoothly. Let's get started!

Preliminaries

How the 90-Minute Process Works

If you were to create your resume on your own, chances are good you would spend hours, even days, coming up with copy and editing it. The beauty of the 90-minute process is that by following clearly defined steps and using another person—your interviewer—as a sounding board, interviewer, and resource, you can produce a better product in a much shorter time.

The 90-minute process consists of six major parts: developing a job target, setting up fact sheets, interviewing for information, translating your notes into resume language, creating a working draft, and perfecting your content.

The time allotted for each part is a general guideline; you may find that you don't need as much or that you need more. The important thing is to take the time you feel you need to successfully complete the step, even if it exceeds the suggested time.

Selecting the Right Interviewer

Now that you have an idea of where the 90-minute process will lead you, you can start your first assignment: identify the right person to help you. He or she might be a friend, former colleague, classmate, brother, or sister. The ideal interviewer is someone who has had the experience of developing his or her own resume, is familiar with the field you have targeted, and has at least as much, if not more, work experience as you. The interviewer should have good oral and written communication skills. As an interviewer, his or her ability to elicit information from you is critical.

The person with whom you are romantically involved may be the most convenient person to recruit as interviewer, but keep in mind that he or she will probably not be as objective in his or her observations or suggestions as someone less involved in your life.

Most important, your interviewer must take the responsibility seriously and be willing to spend 90 minutes to ask good questions and give you thoughtful feedback.

Tools of the Trade

You'll need the following items for the 90-minute process.

- Several pens or pencils.
- At least ten blank sheets of paper (lined or unlined).
- One photocopy of the copy checklist on page 67. (Recommended)
- A typewriter or computer. (Recommended)

Though the section that follows is written for your interviewer, reading it will give you a better understanding of his or her role.

A Crash Course for Interviewers

As interviewer, you are about to play an enjoyable and important role in this unique resume creation process. Just what is expected of you? Two things:

1. Interview the job hunter. Your questions to the job hunter (a list is provided) make the process of getting information down on paper an easy one.

2. Provide feedback and ideas. As you work with the job hunter in choosing words to communicate his or her background and in organizing the

information in a way that can be easily followed, you can act as a sounding board and suggest ways of doing things that may not have otherwise occurred to him or her.

As you offer comments or ask questions, remember:

- *Be encouraging.* Many people feel uncomfortable talking about themselves and their accomplishments, so be sure to put the job hunter at ease by being a good listener and complimenting his or her answers.

- *Don't hesitate to probe.* If you don't understand something the job hunter has said or written, ask for an explanation. Why? Because if the same words make their way into the final version of the resume, the employer who reads the resume is likely to be confused too.

- *Make sure the job hunter doesn't sell himself short.* Job hunters too often prematurely edit their experiences. Your job is to ask questions that will draw out specifics, particularly numbers that will give a job task or an accomplishment a context in which to be better understood.

- *Take notes.* It's difficult for the job hunter to write while speaking, so as you listen, jot down key words and phrases that sound important to you. Before moving on to the next question, read back what you've got. Make suggestions for more effective words or phrases.

- *Direct the conversation.* Part of your job is to keep the interview on track. Don't let the job hunter stray from the question you've asked; simply say, "That's good information, but save it for later because I'll be asking about it." And keep in mind that no one question should take more than a few minutes to answer. If it does, the two of you won't be able to produce a working copy in the 90 minutes allotted.

Interviewer guidelines are interspersed throughout the book to assist you. Be sure to read them before you begin the work described in the corresponding sections. The role you're about to play in helping the job hunter is an important one. Good luck!

Are You an Expert Resume Reviewer?

Before you and your interviewer begin working on your resume, the two of you should take this quiz to find out how good you are at pinpointing resume mistakes. The more aware you are of the things that weaken a resume, the less likely you are to make those same errors on your own.

On a separate piece of paper, identify words, phrases, graphic elements, or sections that you feel are inconsistent, unclear, disorganized, or inconclusive in the resume that appears on the next page. Jot down brief explanations for your choices. There are eleven mistakes and omissions.

```
                     Resume of
                 Edward Christoferson
    26 West 75th Street, NY, NY 10023    (212) 555-8911

    OBJECTIVE: Entry-level job in publishing


    EDUCATION

    New York University Summer Publishing Institute, a
    six-week intensive course in magazine and book
    publishing, Certificate, July 1992

    SUNY Purchase, B.A., 1992, English

    Trinity College, Oxford, England, Summer classes in
    Renaissance History, 1991

    Kenyon College, Gambier, Ohio, Candidate for B.A.,
    1988-89

    Lorain County Community College, Candidate for A.A.,
    1987-88

    Baldwin High School, 1987. Honors student. Sports Editor,
    The Challenger. President, golf club. Captain and
    four-year member of the swim team.


    ACTIVITIES

    Reporter and columnist, The Collegian, 1991-92

    Editor, The Literary Quarterly, 1991

    Member of swim team.


    EXPERIENCE

    Assistant to Product    Pepsico Inc., White Plains,
    Manager, 1990-91           New York
                            Made copies, answered phones,
                            did library research, typed
                            letters

    Bookseller              B. Dalton Books, New York, New York
    Summers, 1989-90        Assisted customers, display
                            work, sales

    Swim Instructor         East Hampton, New York
    Summers, 1987-88        Taught children and adults how
                            to swim
```

Let's see how well you fared. The errors are categorized as content, punctuation and grammar, organization, and design mistakes. Some are much more flagrant than others, but even those that seem trivial can make a resume look less professional.

Content

1. "Resume of" is not necessary. The format of the information tells the reader that this is a resume.
2. Edward's job objective is too general. Because this resume will no doubt only be going out to magazine and book publishers, there's no need to include this information unless it's more specific.
3. The inclusion of colleges that Edward attended but did not receive a degree from (with the exception of the summer program) isn't necessary. In fact, it could work against him because it appears that he couldn't make up his mind about where to attend college. If you are a college graduate, don't include information about your high school unless there is a chance that a potential employer is an alumnus.
4. The single biggest content weakness in this resume is the lack of details under the Activities and Experience sections. The reader can only guess at Edward's level of involvement in what appears to be a student newspaper and a literary magazine. And while Edward is somewhat more specific about his job responsibilities, they come across as being ordinary—there is no mention of any results or accomplishments.

Punctuation and Grammar

1. The acronym SUNY (the second entry under Education) should be spelled out. It can't be

assumed that every reader will know which college it refers to.

2. The names of publications should be underlined or put in quotation marks. For consistency in design, in his revised resume, Edward chose to underline them as he did the names of the other organizations he worked for.

Organization

1. The dates under the Education section get lost in the text. They should be mentioned up front since descriptions are included with the name of the college and program.

2. Edward should consider adding an Interests section. The information listed in it serves as a conversational icebreaker in an interview and gives a prospective employer a glimpse of the kind of person he is.

Design

1. Underlining the Identification section does nothing to enhance the look of this resume. Edward's name should be placed in a more prominent position and set in a larger point size.

2. "Objective" is the only category heading not aligned with the others. They all should be flush left rather than indented. In addition, the heading isn't underlined—it should be for consistency.

3. Overall, the resume is too plain. Too few graphic elements are used.

A round of applause if you caught the majority of these mistakes—you have a keen eye for resume strengths and weaknesses. But don't worry too much if some of these errors eluded your eye. Each of the mistakes described here will be explained in greater detail in the pages ahead.

As you can see on the next page, after using the process described in this book, Edward was able to create a much more descriptive and convincing resume.

Edward Christoferson

26 West 75th Street
New York, New York 10023
(212) 555-8911

OBJECTIVE	Editorial assistant position with a book publisher
EDUCATION	Certificate, July 1992 New York University Summer Publishing Institute, a six-week course in magazine and book publishing B.A., 1992, English, State University of New York at Purchase Trinity College, Oxford, England, summer classes in Renaissance History, 1991

ACTIVITIES

Reporter and columnist
1991–92

The Collegian, weekly school newspaper
• Covered an average of three sporting events weekly, resulting in at least two stories
• Wrote monthly column, "The Sports Observer," which received second-place award in 1991 regional student newspaper competition

Editor
1991

The Literary Quarterly, student-produced quarterly
• Reviewed seventy-five submissions quarterly
• Encouraged student participation by addressing ten creative writing classes; submissions increased 20 percent

EXPERIENCE

Assistant to Product Manager
1990–91

Pepsico, Inc., White Plains, New York
• Produced reports and correspondence on WordPerfect 4.0 (typing speed 80 wpm)
• Corrected grammar and sentence construction in written materials after demonstrating my skills
• Directed telephone calls to appropriate staff members

Bookseller
Summers, 1989–90

B. Dalton Books, New York, New York
• Assisted customers in making book selections
• Set up special displays and monitored inventory
• Received employee of the month award three times

Swim Instructor
Summers, 1987–88

Private pool, East Hampton, New York
Taught approximately 120 children and adults how to swim

INTERESTS

Golf, swimming (competed on high school and college teams)

Creating Your Resume from Scratch

First, Your Fact Sheets

Before you sit down with your interviewer, it's a good idea to put the following headings on separate pieces of blank paper. We'll call them your fact sheets.

Work Experience

Education

Activities

Interests

Fill in factual information under the appropriate headings in advance so that the interviewer will be able to quiz you more effectively—and quickly. If you have a typewriter or, better yet, a computer and word processing software, use it to type in this preliminary information on the fact sheets.

Your **work experience fact sheet** is first. For each job you've held, starting with the most recent, list:

- Your job title(s)
- The employer's name and location (city and state)
- Dates of employment (month and year)

EXAMPLE

—Engineering drafter, Computech, Inc., Norwood, Massachusetts, June 1990–September 1991

Include internships, summer jobs (if you're a student or recent grad), and part-time and unpaid job experiences, as well as full-time positions.

EXAMPLES

—Publicity intern, WNET-TV, New York, New York, Summer 1991

—Switchboard operator, Fort Lauderdale City Hall, Fort Lauderdale, Florida, September 1990–August 1991

On your **education fact sheet** list:

- Name of high school, month and year of graduation (if you've already graduated from college, this information isn't necessary)
- Name of vocational, trade, or technical school; month and year of graduation; name of program completed (if applicable)
- Name of degree received; major; name of college; dates of attendance or month and year of graduation; graduation honors; grade or grade point average if at the B level or better; names of special courses or programs you took abroad, during summer school, or at a specialized school; dates of attendance; certificates or special recognition received. (Note: If you haven't yet graduated, simply put: Candidate, name of degree, date of expected graduation.)

EXAMPLES

—College graduate

B.A., Government, University of Arizona, May 1992

- Cum laude
- Harry S. Truman Scholarship ($7,000 award based on B average and ranking in top 25 percent of class)

—Some college education

Full-time student, Ohio University, 9/1988–12/1990

- Financed 80 percent of college education with 30-hour-per-week job

An Activities section is optional, but it can boost your ratings as a candidate, particularly if you played more important roles in campus or community organizations than you did in your summer or part-time jobs.

On your **activities fact sheet** list:

- Name of clubs, organizations, teams, volunteer activities, or professional organizations for students in which you were an active participant; your role; dates of membership

EXAMPLES

—Student Marketing Association, publicity coordinator, 1990–1991

—UM Women's Golf Team, Captain, 1990–1992

One thing to keep in mind. If you're involved in controversial social or political activities, such as a pro-life or pro-choice group, you're better off omitting your involvement. A prospective employer may not share your view, and that could interfere with your being considered for a job.

In addition, if the activities you are or were involved in are related to the job you hope to land, you may want to list them under a separate heading in your Work Experience section. Create a heading that uses a word related to the field and that sums up the type of skills you have developed. If you hope to land a job as a newswriter for a radio station, for instance, you might want to list your activities as a reporter for the school newspaper and news director for the college radio station under the heading titled "Communications Experience."

An Interests section is also optional. But unless you're a couch potato, it's a good idea to include it. A prospective employer often starts an interview with questions about your interests. Your interests can provide insight into the kind of person you are. And if you and the prospective employer share similar interests, it can help you clinch the job. Remember to be specific.

On your **interests fact sheet** list:
* A few of the activities you enjoy doing in your free time

EXAMPLE

—Windsurfing, collecting antique sports equipment, reading contemporary sports biographies

Develop a Job Objective

Your second advance task is to write down your job target—the position you'd like to land. Whether or not you intend to include it on your resume, you and your interviewer should use the target you write down as the basis for making decisions about which skills and experience to emphasize. The more focused you are about what you want to do and the more knowledgeable you are about the responsibilities of that job and the skills it requires, the easier it will be to develop a resume that will attract the attention of employers you want to work for. The issue of whether it's advisable to include a job objective is discussed in "Create a Working Draft" on page 49.

The more specific and realistic your job objective, the easier it will be to decide what to emphasize on your new resume. If you majored in communications and have worked as an intern for a television program, your job objective might be

* A production assistant for a news or documentary television program

The details of this job description—in particular, the stated interest in news and documentary programming—can be very helpful in highlighting the aspects of this job hunter's experience and skills that support that ambition.

Having more than one job target isn't a problem. In fact, if you're a recent graduate, it's a good idea to consider several related job options. If they aren't closely related, however, you should create several editions of your resume, each of which is geared to a specific target. That can be easily accomplished if you're creating your resume with a word processing or desktop publishing software program.

Next, based on what you know about your target job or jobs, write down at least four or five tasks that someone in that position would be responsible for. This will enable you to make better judgments about what to emphasize from your past jobs or academic experiences.

EXAMPLE

Job Objective: A position as an exercise physiologist at a health club

Job Tasks:

- Evaluate client fitness capabilities
- Design physical fitness improvement programs to help avoid injury and maximize workout benefits for individual clients
- Train clients to use club equipment
- Monitor equipment use and client progress
- Teach weight-training techniques
- Lead aerobics classes
- Encourage and motivate clients to stick with fitness routines

The third step is to identify the two, three, or four areas of expertise under which these job tasks fit. In the example above, these would be evaluation, instruction, and communication. The reason for doing this is to provide a basis for you and your interviewer to analyze how your past academic and work experiences mesh with your target.

If you've never before thought about how to group like sets of skills under a single heading, the following chart can help you. It doesn't contain all areas of expertise— that list would include hundreds of entries. But by looking over the action verbs listed under each area, you'll get a better idea of how skills can be organized by area of expertise. (Areas of expertise are sometimes referred to as functions or functional headings and are used as the main section headings in functional resumes, which are organized by area of expertise.)

Areas of Expertise

Accounting	Administration	Advertising	Coaching
Analyze	Administer	Conceptualize	Coordinate
Audit	Control	Create	Direct
Calculate	Direct	Design	Instruct
Estimate	Institute	Develop	Lead
Examine	Manage	Formulate	Motivate
Plan	Organize	Negotiate	Organize
Project	Oversee	Plan	Schedule
Review	Program	Write	Train

Communications	Design	Finance	Fund-Raising
Conceptualize	Conceptualize	Analyze	Address
Develop	Create	Calculate	Contact
Edit	Develop	Compile	Develop
Interview	Illustrate	Diagnose	Propose
Outline	Lay out	Formulate	Raise
Present	Render	Leverage	Solicit
Research		Negotiate	Write
Write		Research	

Management	Personnel	Public Relations	Research
Administer	Administer	Develop	Analyze
Analyze	Analyze	Market	Calculate
Conduct	Evaluate	Promote	Determine
Control	Interview	Represent	Investigate
Direct	Provide	Research	Solve
Implement	Screen	Speak	Study
Supervise	Test	Write	Test

Undecided About What to Do? Try the Balance-Sheet Approach

If you aren't sure what kind of first job you want you should research your options. There are many ways to do that, among them talking to people in your targeted field whose judgment you trust, taking a short course in making career decisions (many are offered through college placement or career planning offices), or going the self-help route with a career decision-making book such as Richard Nelson Bolles' *What Color Is Your Parachute?*

If you can't decide from among your options, try the balance-sheet approach to making a decision. The concept is easy. You rate the things about a job that are most important to you and give each factor a numerical value. By adding up the score, you can determine which option has the highest rating. Start by making a list of all the possibilities you are entertaining. Then, beginning with the first one, assign a weight (on a scale of one to five, five being the best) to the factors that influence each job's appeal. These include expected salary, ability to work independently, security, variety of job tasks, potential for moving up, work schedule, hours, and any other factors important to you. Add up the points for each one and compare the totals. The job or jobs that get the highest score are the best bets for your next position.

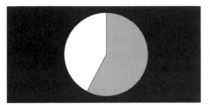

Total time for this exercise:
35 minutes

Ready, Set, Start the Interview

Now it's time to have your interviewer join you.

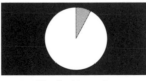

Time for this exercise:
5 minutes

Is Your Job Target on Target?

The first step in the process is to talk about your job target and its tasks so that your interviewer can ask better questions and help you judge what belongs in your resume. Be open to your interviewer's comments and suggestions. He or she may bring up points that haven't occurred to you and may give convincing reasons why you might want to alter your job target or use more than one.

Interviewer Guideline: Make sure you understand the job target. If you're unclear about what the job involves or the required skills, experiences, or credentials, ask the job hunter for more information. If the job hunter can't explain it, suggest that he or she do more research before you continue.

Start the clock, and begin talking. You have 5 minutes.

The Interview

Once you and your interviewer have talked about your job target, you can begin the interview session. The whole point of having the interviewer ask you questions is to have you talk about your work and educational background, which is much easier than writing about it. It's the interviewer's job to ask, "Explain what you mean" or "Can you give me an example?" if he or she doesn't understand your answer. Try to use words that clearly and simply describe your job responsibilities, skills, and accomplishments. Avoid using jargon and technical terms. Keep a pen or pencil in hand at all times. You'll want to jot down words, phrases, and well-expressed ideas as soon as you have answered a question to your interviewer's satisfaction. Taking good notes will make it easier for you to write your resume.

If you have a tape recorder, you may want to tape the session. It will allow you to rewind and play back parts of the interview, which is particularly helpful if something brilliant is said and promptly forgotten.

Time for this exercise:
15 minutes

Work Experience Fact Sheet

Let's start with the work experience fact sheet. When answering the interviewer's questions, try to use numbers, percentages, and amounts to describe how many, how often, or how much. Quantifying what you've done and what you know helps put your accomplishments and skills into perspective for the employer who will be reviewing your resume.

Interviewer Guideline: You should have the job hunter's fact sheets in front of you. Start with the most recently held job and work backward. If the job hunter has already given some thought to what he or she does on the job and what his or her accomplishments have been, you may not need to go beyond the first two questions for each job. The additional questions are suggestions for what to ask if you need to dig deeper. It's crucial to get numbers whenever possible and at least one or two accomplishments or results for each job. Remember to spend more time on those positions that relate to the job target. Treat all kinds of work experience—paid, volunteer, part-time, or full-time—the same way. If the job hunter hasn't had much work experience or experience directly related to the kind of work he or she is applying for, it's particularly important to encourage the person to talk about what he or she has learned and contributed. Take notes as the job hunter speaks. Jot down the verbs and other key words in his or her answers.

Finally, keep the interview on track. Do your best to keep the job hunter from going off on unnecessary tangents.

Put the book aside now, and begin the exercise. You have 15 minutes.

QUESTIONS

- What exactly did you do on your job on a regular (daily, weekly, or monthly) basis? Start with the tasks you consider most important and try to come up with at least five, even if you don't include all of them in your final resume.

- Did any of your accomplishments ever result in a promotion, raise, or other type of recognition? Please describe them and quantify with numbers, for example, a *10 percent* bonus or a *doubling* of your client list.
- Did you manage the work of one or more employees? If so, how many? At what level (clerical, technical, etc.) were those employees?
- What are some of the most important projects you worked on? Briefly describe their purpose and your role. Did you meet or exceed the expectations of your boss (or management)?
- Did you suggest an idea that was successfully implemented by your boss, department, or company? Please describe what it involved, your role in making it work, and any credit or compliments you received as a result.
- Did you train one or more employees to do something you know how to do well? Describe the nature of the task or tasks, whether you did it on your own initiative, and whether others learned how to do it successfully.
- What have you done that has made you feel satisfied or won praise from your boss, management, or clients?

Interviewer Guideline: If the job hunter can't come up with anything, ask how he or she handled an emergency or crisis situation or functioned on the job when the boss wasn't around and whether he or she was complimented on job performance during a review.

• • • •

SAMPLE CONVERSATION

Interviewer: What exactly did you do as a production assistant at WPIX-TV?

Job Hunter: Probably the most important thing I did every day was to check into daily news bulletins and write rough copy for the evening news and weekly magazine programs.

Interviewer: What do you mean when you say "checked into"?

Job Hunter: I called up the sources who were mentioned to verify and add information to what was in the bulletin.

Interviewer: How many news bullctins did you check into every day?

Job Hunter: At least a dozen.

Interviewer: What do you mean by "rough copy"?

Job Hunter: A writer and an editor would usually take what I wrote up and polish it.

What to write down:
- Checked into a dozen news bulletins daily.
- Called up sources to verify and add information.
- Wrote rough copy for writers and editors to polish.

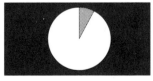

Time for this exercise:
5 minutes

Education Fact Sheet

If you're still enrolled in school or are a recent graduate, your education section should lead off the body of your resume. So let's tackle the education fact sheet next—you've got 5 minutes.

Interviewer Guideline: Start by reading over the information on the education fact sheet. Ask questions about anything that is unclear to you, even if it's a simple detail about the type of degree or certificate received.

QUESTIONS

- Did you work to put yourself through school? If so, what percentage of your education did you pay for?

Interviewer Guideline: If the job hunter has listed any information beyond the name of the degree earned, the program or school, and dates of attendance, ask the following questions.

- How were you selected for the honor, scholarship, or award you've listed? Was it based on grades, leadership ability, or involvement in school organizations? Who made the decision—faculty, administration, officers of the awarding organization, your peers?
- Were others selected or were you the only one?
- Was there a cash award involved? If so, how much?

• • • •

SAMPLE CONVERSATION

Interviewer: You've written down that you received an honor for outstanding academic achievement. What exactly did you do?

Job Hunter: I wrote a term paper that was cited as one of the ten best written by a senior.

Interviewer: That's terrific, especially because good writing skills are a requirement for the position you're applying for. Did someone nominate you for it?

Job Hunter: My history professor submitted it as the best term paper from his department.

Interviewer: Did other departments enter submissions?

Job Hunter: All twenty departments in the arts and sciences division competed. A faculty committee made the decision from among the finalists.

Interviewer: Do you know how many term papers were considered?

Job Hunter: My professor told me it was over 300.

What to write down:

- Wrote one of ten best senior term papers.
- Nominated by history professor.
- Selected by a faculty committee from a field of 20 finalists and over 300 entrants.

Time for this exercise:
5 minutes

Activities Fact Sheet

As your interviewer asks you questions, try to use specifics to describe your involvement in campus or community organizations, sports, or activities.

Interviewer Guideline: If the type of organization is not obvious from its name, ask whether it is a social, professional, community, student government, or other special interest group.

QUESTIONS

- What was the nature and extent of your involvement in the group?

- Did you serve on any committees, participate in planning or executing organization projects, or do fund-raising? What were the results of your efforts?
- Were you an elected or appointed officer of the club or organization? If so, did you serve as a representative of your group? To whom?
- Did you develop any skills related to your job target through your participation?

• • • •

SAMPLE CONVERSATION

Interviewer: What did you do as the copy editor of the yearbook?

Job Hunter: I wrote the lead articles for each section of the book. I helped the editor-in-chief make story assignments. I edited and proofread those assignments when they came in. I also worked with the art director to come up with a design format using Quark Xpress. I made sure all the copy was input correctly into the computer. And I signed off on all the mechanicals.

Interviewer: How much time did this involvement require?

Job Hunter: I spent 15 hours a week on it over a period of eight months.

Interviewer: Did you learn any special skills in this job?

Job Hunter: My copy editing skills really improved, particularly because the yearbook adviser is a former newspaper copy-desk editor. I knew a bit about desktop publishing, but I mastered the Quark Xpress program during the time I used it.

Interviewer: Was the yearbook a success?

Job Hunter: We sold a record number of copies. And the yearbook won an award for superior design from the Student Press Association.

What to write down:

- Wrote lead articles for yearbook sections
- Helped assign stories
- Edited and proofread stories
- Worked with art director to design format
- Supervised copy input
- Signed off on mechanicals
- Sharpened copy editing skills with help of adviser
- Mastered Quark Xpress
- Helped produce yearbook whose sales surpassed school record; won superior-design award from Student Press Association

Time for this exercise:
5 minutes

Interests Fact Sheet

You can move through this part of the interview quickly if you first review your interests fact sheet and select the three most important ones to focus on.

Interviewer Guideline: Aim for specifics about the interests the job hunter has listed and find out whether he or she has only a passing familiarity with them (in which case, they shouldn't be mentioned) or a genuine passion or involvement.

QUESTIONS

- What exactly is your involvement with (the interests listed)?
- How much do you know about it?
- How often do you do it?

• • • •

SAMPLE CONVERSATION

Interviewer: What kind of photography do you like to do?

Job Hunter: Mostly candid shots of interesting people I see on the street. I use black-and-white film, not color.

Interviewer: How long have you been doing it?

Job Hunter: For about ten years. I've taken about a dozen photography workshops.

Interviewer: Do you do your own developing?

Job Hunter: I develop and print my own pictures.

What to write down:

- Take black-and-white candid shots of people.
- Develop and print own pictures.

Time for this exercise:
15 minutes

Total time:
50 minutes

Coming Up with Great Resume Language

Your next task is to consolidate the responsibilities and accomplishments of each job and activity into concise statements. Those related to your job target should be more descriptive than the ones that are not. Don't feel restricted to using the words you have in your notes. If you do, it's very likely that the description of the job responsibility or accomplishment will be too long. In editing each entry on your fact sheets, search for words that will link thoughts or more clearly and concisely convey the task.

Begin each statement with an action verb. Use the past tense unless the task is something you currently do. Avoid making the verb a noun (i.e., using "negotiation skills" instead of "negotiate"). Don't end verbs with "ing."

EXAMPLES

What you've written on your work experience fact sheet:

Checked into a dozen news bulletins daily.

Called up sources to verify and add information.

Wrote rough copy for writers and editors to polish.

How to translate it on your resume:

- Researched a dozen news bulletins daily by calling up sources to verify facts and wrote first-draft news stories

What you've written on your work experience fact sheet:

Take phone calls from dissatisfied or confused customers, an average of fifty a day.

Talk to them without losing my cool.

Have them talk to my supervisor or write up a report to proper department if I can't help them.

Have received more than 100 letters thanking me personally for my help last year.

How to translate it on your resume:

- Help an average of fifty customers who call in daily
- Process or refer complex customer complaints through proper channels
- Have received more than 100 thank-you letters from customers citing my helpfulness and courtesy in the last year

If you're not used to writing on a regular basis, you may find the task of translating your notes into the shorthand language of a resume a bit daunting. But don't worry. Think of the process in terms of the several easy-to-follow formulas:

Formula 1

(A) Action verb (present tense for a current job, past tense for a previously held job) *plus*
(B) Object or people *plus*
(C) To or for whom; of, on, or from what; by, through, or with what

If you need ideas for action verbs, consult the chart on page 40. It contains synonyms for ten action verbs that describe job tasks. For more help in coming up with descriptive action verbs, consult a thesaurus.

EXAMPLES

Dispatched---assignments---to security guards

Monitored---market conditions---for Chicago Mercantile Exchange

Cared for---orphaned infant orangutan

Formula 1 is about as simple as you can get. Don't be afraid to add details if they better explain a job responsibility or accomplishment.

Formula 2

(A) Compound action verbs *plus*
(B) Object quantified and/or described *plus*
(C) To or for whom; of, on, or from what; by, through, or with what *plus*
(D) Descriptor

EXAMPLES

Compiled and wrote---three major state and local news stories---from wire services---for public affairs program

Drafted---legal memoranda and briefs weekly---for senior partners---involved in oil and gas matters

Investigated and reported on---potential employees---for hiring managers---in high-security-clearance areas

Don't feel confined by these formulas; they're merely guidelines for getting your words across clearly and simply.

Calculate	Care for	Coordinate	Decide
Analyze	Administer to	Arrange	Determine
Compute	Attend to	Assign	Evaluate
Estimate	Look after	Organize	Judge
Figure	Serve	Regulate	Select
Take account of	Watch over	Systematize	Weigh
Manage	**Market**	**Mediate**	**Route**
Administer	Deal in	Accommodate	Direct
Head	Sell	Bring to terms	Expedite
Lead	Shop	Pacify	Guide
Oversee		Reconcile	Schedule
Supervise		Settle	Track
Train	**Write**		
Coach	Communicate		
Inform	Compile		
Instruct	Compose		
Teach	Draft		
Tutor			

If your word processing program has a word counting feature, now is a good time to use it to get quick counts of the lengths of your revised job descriptions and accomplishments.

How to Make an Ordinary Job Sound Important

Most people have held ordinary jobs, that is, jobs in which the responsibilities don't seem all that important. But that doesn't mean you can't make what you did—which, if you did a good job, mattered a great deal to your boss and company—*sound* important. It's all in the phrasing. Here are several examples of how it can be done.

EXAMPLES

Laborer, Sonny's Landscaping
— Transported sensitive plants and trees without incurring damage
— Offered tips to customers on how to maintain landscaping
— Scouted location and offered suggestions to customers on placement

Retail clerk, Bloomingdale's
— Rang up between $4,000 and $6,000 in sales transactions daily
— Handled approximately twenty-five customer complaints and returns weekly; usually able to solve without supervisor assistance
— Assisted department managers in buying merchandise and organizing interior displays

Are you ready? Start the clock. You have 15 minutes.

Time for this exercise: Total time:
5 minutes   55 minutes

What Are You an Expert At?

Now it's time to analyze the collection of entries under your Work Experience and Activities sections so that you can identify your areas of expertise. Why is this important?

"Forcing yourself to think about your background in categories of skills, experience, and knowledge helps you mentally organize your thoughts for an interview and is particularly good preparation for answering that often-asked question, 'Tell me about yourself,'" says Richard J. Chagnon, a senior vice president with the Philadelphia-based international outplacement firm, Right Associates. Furthermore, it's a good way to get a handle on which items should be emphasized. You've already identified the areas of expertise required for your job target. The tasks and accomplishments that belong with those headings should be the first ones mentioned under each job entry.

With your interviewer, make a list of the action verbs and the key noun that begin each task or accomplishment on your work experience and activities fact sheets. Then decide which of the three or four areas of expertise required for your targeted job each belongs under. If necessary, you can refer back to step three in "First, Your Fact Sheets" on page 19.

EXAMPLE

Situation: John is a recent graduate who majored in marketing. The following items are descriptions of job tasks he performed in a variety of sports-related part-time or summer jobs and in school activities. His job target is to sell advertising space for a sports publication. The three main areas of expertise he has identified for that target are: communications, market research, and sales.

List of tasks, skills, activities

Assisted sports director and weekend anchor in gathering sports information, logging it in, covering sports events, and interviewing sports personalities in Buffalo area— *communications*

Supervised swimmers and enforced rules at college pool during free-swim times— *not applicable*

Identified successful alumni business owners (potential corporate donors) through library and phone research— *market research*

Assisted in all phases of expanding readership of local sports publication; circulation increased 10 percent in six months— *sales*

Persuaded previous alumni donors to increase their donations and persuaded alumni who never donated to pledge; surpassed $5,000 goal by $2,500— *sales*

Targeted prospective advertisers for the special sales department of radio station— *market research*

Served as a parking lot attendant at sports complex— *not applicable*

Interviewed coaches and team players and developed sports stories for student newspaper— *communications*

Sold outdoor products for home-center chain; twice nominated salesperson of the month— *sales*

John should highlight the tasks and accomplishments that he identified as being a communications, market research, or sales area of expertise. If he chooses to mention the two items that don't fit under these categories, he should feature them less prominently. In a chronological resume, he can highlight his tasks and accomplishments by positioning them as the first entries under their respective jobs. The resume reader is likely to read the first and second bullets under each job. If they're interesting, the reader will pay more attention to the ones that follow. If not, he or she may skip over those others.

Again, the clearer you make the connection between your skills and accomplishments and the areas of expertise in the targeted job, the easier it'll be for an employer to recognize that you are a viable candidate.

The clock is ticking. You have 5 minutes!

The Format Issue

A chronological resume is still the preferred format and with good reason—it's the most readily understood, reader-friendly format. Education credentials and job experience are arranged in a time line, starting with the most recent and going backward, ultimately listing the first job last. People who spend much of their work day reviewing resumes—personnel agency counselors, executive recruiters, and human resources staff—are partial to the chronological format because it makes their job easier. It clearly identifies dates, job titles, and the names of employers. Chronological resumes are also preferred because the placement of dates next to facts makes reference checking simple.

You should choose the chronological format if you're looking for your first job after attending or graduating from high school, community college, four-year college, or graduate school. It's a good choice because with it employers can get a handle on the skills you have based on your major and your summer and part-time work experiences.

The second format, a functional resume, is less widely accepted and understood by employers. In it, the main section is composed of areas of expertise followed by a brief work history section and an education section. It is best used by career changers. However, if you feel you can come across as a stronger candidate by using a functional resume, consult "Resume Makeovers," which begins on page 95, for examples and instructions on how to write one.

The third format option is a combination chronological/functional resume. The primary advantage of a functional resume, its analysis of your strengths by area of expertise, is added to a chronological resume, often as a second page. Why use this format? It's a way to emphasize groups of skills or experience that can help the resume reader more readily see why you are qualified for a position.

Other books on writing resumes include the analytical (or targeted) format, which presents what the job hunter knows and what he or she has done as individual skills and achievements grouped under headings such as "Capabilities" and "Accomplishments." I've decided against presenting this option because most employers don't know what to make of it. And if an employer is having a difficult time getting a handle on you as a candidate, he or she is likely to put your resume aside (and perhaps never get back to reviewing it further) or to put it immediately in the reject pile.

Another problem with an analytical resume is that it doesn't lend itself to easily identifying when the job hunter used the skills or accomplished the results he or she has listed. The reason cited most often for using this format—defining experiences so that they fit a specific position—can, I'm convinced, be done more easily and just as effectively with one of the other three formats. You can find examples of all three in "Resume Makeovers."

Time for this exercise:
25 minutes

Total time:
80 minutes

Create a Working Draft

Congratulations—you're entering the home stretch. The next step—editing your fact sheets into a legible working draft—is gratifying because you see the results of your efforts so far.

Using a computer is the best way to compose a draft, but a typewriter is a good second choice. Whoever is the most proficient keyboarder—you or your interviewer—should input the copy. The other person should watch as the copy is keyed to correct errors and make final editing suggestions. If neither a computer nor a typewriter is available, neatly transfer the copy onto a single sheet of paper so that it will be easy to follow.

Don't be concerned at this stage if your resume exceeds one page. You won't know for sure whether all of the copy can comfortably fit in the space you'd like until you've designed it.

With a chronological format, sections of information should be listed in the following order.

- Identification (name, address, phone number)
- Job Objective (optional)
- Summary of Qualifications (optional)
- Education
- Work Experience

- Activities or Professional Involvements/Affiliations (optional)
- Skills (optional)
- Interests

The exception to this sequence is the resume of a job hunter with full-time job experience that postdates attending school or receiving a degree. In that case, the Work Experience section should come before the Education section.

Read the information under each section here before you begin to finalize your copy for the corresponding section on your resume.

Identification

- Your full name (a formal name rather than a nickname)
- Your permanent address (street number and name, apartment number, city, state, and zip code). If you have more than one address because you're a student or someone who lives away from home part of the year, indicate which is your permanent address. You might also want to include the dates you can be reached at both addresses as the last line of information in this section.

EXAMPLE

OWEN EDWARDS

984 Beresford Road	6110 N. Elm Street
Jamestown, PA 32098	Syracuse, NY 10967
215-555-9078	518-555-0091
(Temporary Address	(Permanent Address)
4/92–8/92)	

- Your phone number. It must be one where you (or someone who can take a message for you) are available during working hours. If there are times when no one is home, consider investing in an answering machine or hiring a telephone answering service (now available through some local telephone companies). List your work number if you can comfortably accept a phone call, however brief, from a prospective employer.

No other personal information—social security number, birth date, marital status, number of dependents, health status, height, weight, or other physical characteristics—should be included. These details are unnecessary and some may cause you to be ruled out.

Job Objective

Even though you have a written job target, which was used to help you develop the content of your resume, it may not be necessary or advisable to include it on the resume itself. Before you decide whether it makes sense in your case, consider some pros and cons.

Pro: A job objective is useful when sending your resume to an employer who is receiving resumes for more than one type of position (almost always the case with personnel departments and departments or divisions of large firms). In short, a job objective is a good way to route a resume to the right person or pile.

Con: A job objective that states the obvious is unnecessary and takes up space. If you're only sending your resume to the type of employer you have targeted in your objective, you may as well eliminate it.

Pro: A job objective can be useful to the resume reviewer if you hope to do anything that is inconsistent with your educational credentials. It's necessary, of course, to support that objective with skills or experience acquired through jobs or activities.

Con: An objective that's specific may narrow your options. If your objective states that you're looking for a position as an editorial assistant at a magazine and there are no such openings at the magazines you've applied to, you may not be considered for other equally good entry-level positions in the production or fact-checking departments. Your job objective should be broad enough to include related entry-level job areas.

If you decide to include a job objective on your resume, keep the following in mind.

- Speak not of what your employer can do for you, but what you can do for an employer.

EXAMPLE

Self-serving job objective:

A creative position in which I can fully utilize my artistic and design skills and gain more direct client experience.

Employer-focused job objective:

A position in a graphic arts department that would allow me to contribute my artistic and design experience to projects that would enhance the firm's relationships with clients.

- Be cautious in your use of self-attributed qualities.

EXAMPLE

Self-congratulatory wording:

A challenging position that is commensurate with my excellent writing and editing skills.

Better use of self-attributed strengths:

An entry-level position in corporate communications that requires a strong background in proofreading, grammar, and writing basics.

- Avoid overused adjectives and phrases that provide no useful information.

EXAMPLE

A creative, self-motivated individual seeks the opportunity to grow within a progressive organization.

- Don't talk about your long-term goals. Mentioning them can be counterproductive, particularly if you say that you'd eventually like to be boss or to start your own business.

Summary of Qualifications

The cover letter has traditionally been the place where the job hunter has summarized his or her skills, experiences, and, sometimes, personal qualities. In recent years, however, this information has begun to appear at the top of resumes right after the identification or job objective. Presumably, it's a way to flag the attention of those who may see the resume but not the cover letter. But is it an effective use of space? It all depends on what you say and how you say it. General statements about your work habits and personality qualities are a waste of space.

EXAMPLE

Strong interpersonal skills. Proficient organizational skills and good attention to detail. Able to anticipate problems before they arise. Self-motivated, able to work under pressure.

A short, fact-filled summary with statements or examples that back up claims about your abilities, on the other hand, can be effective.

EXAMPLE

- Four summers of experience working as a reservations agent for a major hotel chain
- A bachelor's degree in hotel and restaurant management
- Fluent in Spanish and French
- In the words of my supervisor: "Works comfortably with the sophisticated business client and the leisure travel client; maintains a sense of humor under pressure."

Education

Start with the last school you attended or graduated from and list each entry in reverse chronological order, naming the first one you attended last. Remember, it's not necessary to include every school you ever attended. Entries should start with either the name of your degree or the name of the college. Each should include

- University name. If the location isn't obvious from the name or its reputation, provide the city and state.
- Degree received. A.A., B.A., B.S., M.B.A., and Ph.D. are all easily recognized degrees; other degrees should be spelled out unless you are certain the initials will be recognized by people in the field in which you are job hunting. If you are enrolled in a program but haven't received your degree yet, you can express your status by including the date of expected graduation.

EXAMPLE

B.A., History, Ohio University, Athens, Ohio
Date of Expected Graduation: December 1992

- Year degree was received. If you didn't receive a degree or aren't sure of when you'll graduate, you should indicate that you're a candidate for a degree and mention the years you were enrolled in the program or the number of hours you have completed.

EXAMPLE

Candidate, M.A., Teacher's College, Columbia University
Have completed 45 of 60 hours required

- Major field of study, grade point average (if it's 3.0 or higher), and significant honors (i.e., graduating with distinction or Phi Beta Kappa). If you received more than one honor, award, or scholarship, you could create a subheading and list each item under it.

EXAMPLES

Baruch College, New York, New York, A.A., Accounting, 1992, GPA 3.5

B.A., Philosophy, Georgetown University, Washington, D.C., 1992
$500 Top Departmental Thesis Award

B.S., Civil Engineering, Miami University, Oxford, Ohio, 1992

Honors: Full scholarship based on SAT scores and high school GPA
Book scholarship from National Society of Women Engineers based on student project for national competition

- Percentage of education you personally financed through scholarships, part-time work, or summer jobs. This kind of statement shows that you're a motivated person and that you can successfully juggle more than one commitment at a time—both highly prized qualities in today's workplace.

EXAMPLE

B.A., Home Economics, Foothill College, Los Altos, CA, 1992
Financed 90 percent of educational expenses through part-time and summer jobs

- Special programs of study. If you spent a summer or semester studying or working in another country or in a special program, describe it briefly after you mention the name of the school and program. Be sure to mention the criterion used for your selection to the program (i.e., grades).

EXAMPLE

Summer, 1991, Hebrew University, Jerusalem, Israel
Studied Hebrew and Biblical literature and spent one month living and working on a kibbutz

- If you have received a certificate or degree for completing a program *after* you graduated from college or high school, that information should appear above the college or high school information. You can emphasize the importance of a program by adding numbers or a short description.

EXAMPLE

Certificate in Computer Technology, 1985
Merritt College, Oakland, CA (full-time two-year program)

Listing courses you took isn't necessary. However, if they're relevant to the position you're looking for, you can mention them in a cover letter.

Work Experience

"Work Experience" is one of the most popular headings. Other options for this section include employment, business history, work history, experience, employment experience, professional experience, and professional background. You might want to create one category for work experience that is related to your job target (i.e., Communications Experience) and another called Other Work Experience or Summer and Part-Time Jobs. The following information should be part of each job subheading.

- Job title
- Company name
- Dates of employment

Including the company location (city and state) may be important if you've worked in more than one geographic area. It's *not* necessary to include:

- Headings that state categories (i.e., Job Title, Dates of Employment, Name of Employer)

- Address or phone number of the employer or the name and job title of your manager (they can be included on a separate reference sheet).

If your job titles reflect the fact that you have worked in a number of related jobs in the field you have targeted, make them the most prominent piece of information.

EXAMPLE

Work Experience

Assistant Technical Writer, Information Services, Inc., Wellesley, Massachusetts, Summer 1991

If your job titles don't tell as impressive a story as the names of your employers, position that information first.

EXAMPLE

Work Experience

<u>AT&T</u>, Customer Service Representative, Basking
   Ridge, New Jersey, Summers 1990–1991

Placing dates of employment flush left, instead of having them follow the name or location of the employer, and indenting the other components is a good choice if you want to emphasize your work continuity.

EXAMPLE

Work Experience

Summers   <u>Hotel reservations agent</u>, Hilton Hotels
1989–present   International, Chicago, Illinois

If you have worked in several positions at one company, it's best to mention the company name and location first, then list your titles and the dates you worked in those positions.

EXAMPLE

Work Experience

<u>J.C. Penney Co.</u>, Houston, Texas
   Assistant to special events coordinator, 1991–present
   Department manager, 1991
   Retail sales clerk, 1989–1990

If the company or companies you worked for are small and/or not likely to be known to the people reviewing your resume, it's smart to add a short description of the company after its name. Another way to handle this is to work the company description into the sentence that describes your responsibilities and accomplishments.

EXAMPLE

Customer Service Representative, Childcraft (a mail-order catalog featuring educational toys), Denver, Colorado, November 1988 to present

To ensure that you get the maximum information in the minimum space, carefully edit your entries under each job. Look for repetition. It's most likely to occur in your description of job tasks. Decide where it's most appropriate and delete the second reference.

If, for example, you started as an assistant preschool teacher but earned your teacher certification and later worked as a head preschool teacher, a job task applicable to both is

- Prepared materials for arts-and-crafts projects

Instead of repeating that task when you describe the higher-level job, make it implicit in the description of a similar higher-order job task.

- Developed arts-and-crafts projects, delivered carefully thought through directions and supervised children in project execution

Tighten your draft by eliminating unnecessary words. All of the following are unnecessary.

- Responsible for
- Worked as a (job title)
- Know how to do
- Experienced in
- Involved in
- Conversant in (or with)

Incorporate accomplishments as clauses in the description of your job tasks.

- Explained membership benefits to potential health club clients, efforts that resulted in fifty new members in ten months

Skills

You've probably mentioned specific skills when describing your job responsibilities. Highlighting these in a separate section is optional, but it's a good idea if they're essential to landing the job you want. It may help to give the section a more specific title—Technical Skills or Hardware and Software Skills or Office Equipment Skills.

If you list the names of equipment or software programs, be sure to include the version that you work on (Microsoft Word 4.0). And be sure to get the spelling and capitalization of the words right; product names often defy the rules.

Define your skill level if it makes sense to do so. "Can type 80 wpm," or "Able to write, speak, and translate Russian."

Activities

Including activities is always a good idea if you have space. It shows what you are interested in. How many you choose to include and the detail you provide is a judgment call. This section may be as long as the Work Experience section if you've been very active in campus organizations. If you decide to include an Activities section, it's important to select a heading that announces the kind of information you are presenting. Some of the possibilities are:

- Extracurricular Activities
- Professional Activities
- Professonal Memberships
- Community Activities
- Civic Activities
- Volunteer Work

One of the best ways to give a capsule view of your activities is to list the type of affiliation you have (member, officer, committee chair), the name of the organization (and, if necessary, a brief explanation of what it is), and the dates of your involvement.

EXAMPLE

Secretary, Undergraduate Speech Communication Association, 1991–92

Captain, Men's Soccer Team, University of Oklahoma, 1991–92 season

Another option is to start each involvement with an action verb that describes something you did or accomplished.

EXAMPLE

- Mobilized 100 volunteers to design, build, paint, and assemble stage sets for five major productions
- Coordinated successful campaign of first-time city council member in a race the press described as a "shoo-in" for the incumbent

It's also acceptable to place activities that are directly related to your targeted job under an experience heading that defines the area of expertise, for example, Communications Experience or Counseling Experience. The fact that the experience was an internship or volunteer activity doesn't matter. What's more important is to emphasize that you have accumulated experience in your job target area.

EXAMPLE

Situation: A recent college graduate with a B.A. in English who hopes to land an account executive position with a tour operator might include the following activity in a section titled "Travel and Tourism Experience."

Trip Organizer, Student Activities Organization, Michigan State University, 1991–92

- Organized and supervised a spring break tour to Fort Lauderdale

61

- Collected 150 reservations and deposits
- Made hotel room assignments and performed room inspections
- Provided entertainment during 10-hour bus trip
- Net profit to Student Activities was $3,500

Interests

Some people question whether to include a line or two of information that's not related to their work lives. But employers, recruiters, and outplacement people I have consulted say "Do it." Why? Because it's the one place to give the reader of your resume insight into who you are beyond your work identity. More than that, it provides a casual way for the interviewer to start a conversation. And it just may be that the employer shares one of your interests, which can only help you as a candidate. If you have an unusual interest, for example, playing guitar in a Celtic music group or competing in hot-air-balloon races, it may just capture the fancy of the resume reader and result in his or her wanting to learn more about you.

A simple list of interests, even if it consists of only two items, is fine. It's important to be specific. Saying that you enjoy fashion, films, sports, or traveling is not very revealing. It's far better to say: Shopping for vintage-clothing bargains, attending major film festivals, watching major league baseball, or taking train trips. Another way to define your interests is to put a few words of explanation after each item.

EXAMPLES

Karate (have earned a yellow belt)

Playing the piano (have a regular one-night engagement each weekend at a local restaurant)

Black-and-white photography (develop and print own photos)

References

It's not necessary to include the line "References Available on Request"—that's a statement of the obvious. You may, however, want to prepare a list of references on a separate piece of paper so that you can give it to a prospective employer once he indicates you are in the running for a job. That could be as early as the end of a first interview, which is a good reason to take the reference sheet with you. At the top of the sheet, use the same identification heading as you did for your resume. Then center the heading "List of References." Include the following information for each reference you give: the person's name, his or her job title, phone number, and the name and address of the company. Including the names of professors is not particularly helpful, since the professor/student relationship is much different from that of the employer/employee. But a faculty member who is familiar with your work habits because of his or her advisory role to a campus organization or activity in which you were involved is fine to list.

EXAMPLE

Andrew Amore

150 Lakeview Drive
Chicago, Illinois 60606
312-555-1058

List of References

Robert Johnson, Vice President, Taxes
Sara Lee Corporation
Three First National Plaza
Chicago, Illinois 60604
312-555-2600

One statement that you may want to include at the bottom of your resume is "Willing to Relocate" (if you are).

Being flexible about where you live may result in being considered for a job in a location other than the one you have applied for.

Why You Shouldn't Tell White Lies

You may be tempted to inflate your job title, fudge dates of employment, or exaggerate educational credentials on your resume in order to come across as a more qualified job candidate. It's *not* a good idea.

Altering the truth can get you into trouble. Employers often take the time to check information on resumes. If a prospective employer discovers inconsistencies, he or she is likely to bump you off the list immediately. The reasoning? If you lie about your credentials, how can you be trusted as an employee? If the discovery is made after you've been hired, you stand to lose your job. In short, the edge you think you may gain isn't worth the risk.

There *are* ways to present yourself as a strong candidate without telling white lies and jeopardizing your credibility, however. Avoid the temptations listed below by following the accompanying suggestions.

- *Changing job titles.* The risk of inflating your job title to make your job and responsibilities sound more important than they really are (or were) is that it's easy to get caught. Job titles are one of the few things that personnel departments routinely provide to prospective employers who inquire. If, however, your title doesn't accurately reflect the scope and importance of your responsibilities, you can alter it to make it more accurately reflect what you do. To avoid the possibility of any misunderstanding, you should clarify the change at your interview—mention that your actual job was X, but that you took the liberty of making it clearer in the wording on your resume.

- *Inventing academic credentials.* It's downright dangerous to claim you attended or graduated from a particular school if you didn't—just as bad is awarding yourself a degree you never earned. If a help-wanted ad or posted job requires a certain educational background, be honest about your credentials and explain in your cover letter why you should nonetheless be considered.

- *Exaggerating your capabilities.* Being self-confident is a plus, but overstating your knowledge or expertise on paper not only may cause embarrassment if you're asked a technical question during the interview but may result in your being written off as a fraud.

- *Taking more credit than is yours.* It's fine to describe your contributions to a successful project, but saying that you initiated, supervised, or were solely responsible for something when that was not really the case is foolish. It's too easy for a prospective employer to discover what your real role was through a conversation with your former boss, colleagues, or people you both know. At the very least, your credibility will suffer; and in the worst-case scenario, you'll be dismissed as a candidate.

- *Claiming free-lance status.* You should claim such status only if you really were engaged in such efforts; otherwise, you won't have legitimate answers about questions an employer is likely to ask about your "business."

Once you have put together your working draft, you're in the home stretch. Turn the page and begin fine tuning your resume.

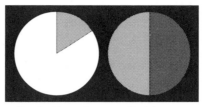

Time for this exercise: Total time:
10 minutes   90 minutes

Perfect Your Copy

The final step before you design your resume is to make sure that the copy is in its best final form. You and your interviewer should go through the following checklist together and look for and mark omissions, repetitions, misspellings, and typographical errors. If you're unsure about the rationale or options for any of the items mentioned on the checklist, go back to "Create a Working Draft" on page 49.

If you're working on a computer, use the word processing program's spell-checking feature to spot typographical and spelling errors, and double check by reading through it. After all, if "to" is keyed instead of "two," it will not be caught by the spell checker because while the usage is incorrect, the spelling is correct.

Copy Checklist

IDENTIFICATION INFORMATION

What's needed:

☐ Full name
☐ Address (temporary and permanent with dates)
☐ Daytime phone number

What isn't needed:

Social security number
Marital status
Number of dependents
Height, weight, and other physical characteristics
Work availability
Health status
Date of birth

JOB OBJECTIVE
(Optional)

What's needed:

☐ Short statement (no more than two lines) in clear, specific language

SUMMARY OF QUALIFICATIONS
(Optional)

What's needed:

☐ Precise listing of skills or areas of expertise
☐ Personal qualities backed up by examples or attributed by others
☐ Three-line maximum

SECTION HEADINGS

What's needed:

☐ Correct sequence
☐ Consistency in placement

EDUCATION

What's needed:

☐ Name of certificate/degree received and year/month awarded

☐ Major field of study
☐ Name of school (location if not apparent from name)
☐ Major scholarships/awards received
☐ Honors received
☐ Percentage of college expenses earned through summer or part-time jobs

What's not needed:

Course work (unless recent and relevant to position you are applying for)

WORK EXPERIENCE

What's needed:

☐ Clauses, not complete sentences
☐ Current job responsibilities in present tense (except in functional format—use past tense)
☐ Past job responsibilities in past tense
☐ Acronyms or abbreviations spelled out
☐ Different action verbs so none appears more than once

What's not needed:

Employer phone number
Name of supervisor
The phrases "responsible for" or "duties included"
The headings "position," "job title," or "duties"
Capitalizing words unnecessarily
Redundant job tasks
References to salary
Reasons for leaving past job

Accomplishments

What's needed:

☐ Job, time frame, or context in which each occurred

☐ Numbers to quantify
☐ Solid analysis of results
☐ Specifics
☐ Examples

What's not needed:

Self-congratulatory wording

ACTIVITIES
(Optional)

What's needed:

☐ Name of organization (several-word explanation if necessary)
☐ Brief description of role you played
☐ Dates of involvement
☐ Accomplishments (with numbers to quantify)

SKILLS
(Optional)

What's needed:

☐ One- or two-word description of skill and skill level
☐ Correctly spelled names of software programs, hardware, or other equipment

INTERESTS

What's needed:

☐ Brief descriptions of specific activities

As you no doubt noticed, your 90 minutes are up. Congratulations for working through the process! Your content should be in perfect condition. Space may ultimately dictate decisions about whether to include or leave out certain entries. You'll still have an opportunity to cut material once you have designed your resume—the next step.

Design Your Resume

What your resume says is important, but unless it looks inviting, it may not get more than a glance from potential employers. Until a few years ago, it was fine to type your resume and have it reproduced on bond paper—the number of job hunters who had their resumes typeset was low. Now, however, more and more job hunters are using word processing or desktop publishing programs to produce resumes with presentations that make their typed counterparts look like plain cousins.

A graphically pleasing resume is worth the extra time or money to produce, particularly when competition for jobs is keen. Making your resume a visual success is something you can easily do, particularly if you know a word processing program such as Microsoft Word or WordPerfect and can access a computer. If you don't, there are two options: Pay someone to input it for you, or rent a computer at a copy shop that has resume design templates available and input it yourself. Many copy shops, including AlphaGraphics and Kinko's, both of which have franchises nationwide, will design resumes from handwritten or typed copy. They can also design resumes from copy that has already been input on a disk, which reduces the chance of the designer making typographical errors and may cost less since inputting copy is time consuming. Fees for this service vary across the country but on the average range from $30 to $90 for a one-page resume and $40 to $110 for a two-page resume. Some copy shops will also sell you a duplicate disk with your resume on it for a minor charge, which enables you to update it on disk whenever necessary. Be sure to ask what word processing or desktop publishing program—and which version—was used to create the resume document, and label the disk.

The second option, using a resume template and inputting the copy yourself, is available at AlphaGraphics. Doing this requires no computer know-how, just keyboarding skills. You pay by the hour to use a Macintosh—the rate ranges from $8 to $20. If you're not a good typist, keep in mind that keying it yourself could end up costing you more than having a design specialist do the whole job.

If you've decided to have someone else design your resume, skip ahead to "How to Get Your Resume into the Hands of Decision Makers" on page 85.

Resume Length

I prefer a one-page resume because it shows the job hunter knows how to highlight and organize material, and there's no chance that the second page will be lost if the staple or paper clip doesn't hold. Today's word processing and desktop publishing programs allow you to get a lot of copy on a single page and still have a great-looking resume.

A Primer on Design

You don't need to be a graphic designer to design a terrific-looking resume. If you know little or nothing about design, however, you may inadvertently make a beginner's mistake, such as using more than one typeface. But knowing a lot about design can get you in trouble, too, because you may be tempted to show off your expertise and overdo it.

"Keep one word in mind as you lay out your resume—KISS—or 'keep it simple, stupid,'" says Barbara Stafford, a graphic designer and manager of the electronic graphics department at AlphaGraphics' commercial printing division. "The challenge is to make the text inviting and readable, not to dazzle the resume reader with fancy graphic sleights of hand," she adds.

Her advice makes a lot of sense; after all, a resume is as highly developed a form as a business letter. Here's how to create a great-looking resume in six steps:

Select the right typeface and point size. You may be limited in your choice of typeface or font by what is available on the software program you are using. Microsoft Word, for example, offers a choice of eight typefaces. Typefaces that are not included in your software can be purchased separately and added to it. You may choose a serif font, which features short cross lines at the ends of the main strokes of the letters, or a sans serif font, which does not.

EXAMPLE

Serif font: Md   *Sans serif font:* Md

The following list of typefaces is highly recommended for resumes. The names may differ slightly (i.e., Times, Times Roman, or Times New Roman), depending on the company that produced the type for the software program, and they may look slightly different but not enough to be noticed by an untrained eye.

Serif Fonts

Times—a condensed typeface that's a good choice if you need to get a lot of text on a page.

New Century Schoolbook—a wide typeface that's a good choice if you want to expand your text and fill out a page.

Palatino—a typeface that's more distinctive than its close relative, Times.

Bookman—another wide typeface that's a good choice if you want to expand your text and fill out a page.

Sans Serif Fonts

Helvetica and Helvetica Narrow—a legible, clean typeface with a simple design; Helvetica Narrow allows you to get more text on the page.

Optima—a thick and thin typeface that's distinctive and not as widely used as other typefaces mentioned here.

Univers—the equivalent of Helvetica and Helvetica Narrow for IBM PCs and compatibles.

Avoid using a script font, because it is too hard to read.

EXAMPLE

It's best to avoid a script font

The point size—the specification for the size of the type—should be a 10- or 12-point size for the body of your resume. You might start with 10 point if you think you'll have trouble getting everything on one page. You shouldn't go smaller than a 9-point size, or some resume readers will have to strain to make out the letters.

Headings should be a consistent size and be in proportion to the text size. Use a 14-point size for all headings if you use 12 point for the text, use a 12-point size if you use 10 point for the text. Avoid the temptation to enlarge your name to a huge point size that will look disproportionate. An 18-point size is the largest you should use for your name if you use 14-point headings. A 14-point size is fine if you use 12-point headings. Subheadings (job title, employer, degree earned, college attended) should be set in the same point size as the text that follows it.

Be consistent about the placement of section headings. You can pull the resume reader's eye to your name by centering it on the page. Your address can go directly underneath. If you are listing more than one address, you may want to put one on the left side and one on the right and indicate the dates when you can be reached at each.

Because we read from left to right, it makes aesthetic and practical sense to position all your headings flush left. Centered headings are less desirable. All entries under all subheadings should be indented the same amount of space. Second or wraparound lines may be indented more.

Keep graphic elements minimal. To highlight your headings, use boldface, capital letters, italic (only if it is easy to read), or underline. If you're creating a functional resume, incorporate a slightly different graphic element for the areas of expertise than you use for other headings.

EXAMPLE

Main headings:	Areas of expertise:
WORK HISTORY	**Communication**
EDUCATION	**Research**
INTERESTS	**Public Speaking**

For subheadings (job title, employer, dates of employment), use only one or two of the four elements suggested here. Using three elements at a time—for instance, underlining, italic, and boldface—is overkill. Avoid outlining or shadowing letters; they make copy hard to read.

EXAMPLE

Work Experience
<u>Computer Entry Clerk</u>, Savin Corporation, Stamford, Connecticut, 1990–1991

Each entry under a subheading should be indented and set off with a simple graphic element so that the eye can move quickly and easily down the page. Blocks of copy that use only periods as punctuation are more difficult to read. Bullets are a good way to introduce items under headings, providing they do not dwarf the size of the type.

Dashes, triangles, or squares are fine for setting off copy too, but avoid the temptation to use the many icons and symbols that software makes available, such as snowflakes, stars, or pointing fingers. They detract from the simplicity and form of a resume.

EXAMPLE

Work Experience
<u>Computer Entry Clerk</u>, Savin Corporation, Stamford, Connecticut, 1990–1991

- Researched machine status; acted as group troubleshooter when problems arose
- Assisted with training new personnel

The only place a line across the whole page belongs, should you choose to use one, is after the identification section and before the first major heading.

EXAMPLE

Leah Hanson
10 Johnson Road
Rahway, NJ 07389
(201) 555-3190

EXPERIENCE

Using a border to frame your copy is a mistake, say graphic designers. It pulls the eye of the reader away from the text, which should be the main attraction.

Build in white space. The easiest way to make sure your resume doesn't look too cluttered is to allow a 1-inch margin on all four sides and to create what's known in design as leading (extra space) between your headings. The greatest leading should be between the Identification section and the first heading.

If you have plenty of white space to manipulate, it's preferable to have more space at the bottom than at the top. Don't increase the leading between headings, or your resume will look too spread out. For most people, the problem will be too little space. If that's what you've found, reducing the margins to a half inch all around may increase what you can get on a page. If you try this and it doesn't work, you can reduce the point size (from 12 to 10 or 10 to 9) and bring the margins back to 1 inch. If that doesn't work, reduce the margins again. Remember, don't go smaller than a 9-point type size or set less than one-half-inch margins. It's better to cut copy or create a second page.

Make a sophisticated paper choice. There are three elements to consider: weight, finish, and color. The most commonly used resume papers are 20-pound bond or 50-pound offset (both weigh the same) in a linen (textured) or laid (flat) finish.

If you want the Mercedes Benz of the paper world, go for a 24-pound Nekoosa, Classic Linen, or Becket Cambric. A 24-pound paper is thicker and has more texture than 20-pound bond or 50-pound offset. Don't go overboard in your search for a paper that will stand out in the crowd. A heavy cover stock or gloss finish, for example, will stand out, but for the wrong reasons. Ditto for color choices other than neutral ones. Different shades of white, grey, and beige are classy and show sophistication.

The best way to decide on a paper is to ask your local copy shop to show you the ones mentioned above and other similar papers. Whatever your choice, you should buy extra sheets of the same paper to use for cover letters. Envelopes should also match.

Reproduce your resume so that each one looks like an original. The best choices are the high-quality professional copiers used in copy shops (for large quantities) and laser printers (especially if you intend to customize individual resumes, send out a limited quantity, or have produced several resumes, each with a different job target).

Final Design Dos and Don'ts

- DO strive for consistency in your use of graphic elements. For example, if you capitalized your first job title, subsequent job titles should also be capitalized.
- DO insist on proofreading the final copy several times (and have someone else whose judgment you trust do the same) *before* it's printed.
- DO use black ink.
- DON'T mix typefaces.
- DON'T produce a two- or four-color resume to show off your design repertoire.
- DON'T use screened images behind the type.
- DON'T include a photograph unless you are an actor or actress.

A Word on Unique Resumes

Unique resumes can get an employer's attention. And sometimes they favorably impress an employer. But the arguments against trying to create a unique resume are powerful. (1) Unless you have graphic design training, your efforts are likely to look amateurish. (2) Your unique design (an oversize resume, for example) may prove problematic because it doesn't easily fit in a resume stack. Set aside, it may be forgotten or trashed. (3) Your attempt to be clever, avant-garde, or humorous may be misinterpreted.

One eager applicant who hoped to land a public relations job with a firm in Reno, Nevada, laid out the content of his resume so that it formed the shape of the state of Nevada. His resume didn't get past the first cut because it was too cute.

Your time will probably be better spent doing basic job search legwork: identifying potential employers, meeting with people in those organizations who are in a position to advise or help you, and contacting decision makers by sending your resume, a carefully thought-out cover letter, and following up with a phone call.

Putting Your
Resume to Work

How to Get Your Resume into the Hands of Decision Makers

Once the final version of your resume is reproduced, you'll be armed with your most important job-hunting tool: You. Now that you have analyzed your skills and accomplishments on paper, you should feel more confident about discussing them with potential employers.

Based on hundreds of interviews with employers, recruiters, employment counselors, and job hunters over the last twenty years, I believe that a well-written resume can be extremely helpful in a job search whether it is used to get an interview, to familiarize those involved in the hiring process with who you are, or to follow up an interview.

Too often, however, job hunters use their resume as a crutch. They figure if they send out enough copies to employers, someone somewhere is going to say, "This is the perfect person for us." No way, José. Getting an interview isn't that easy, at least not usually. You'll have far more success if you're highly selective about where and to whom you send your resume—identifying companies, divisions, departments, and people who have a need for someone with your skills and background.

Responding to help-wanted ads is fine, but you can't afford to make that the focus of your efforts. It's essential for you to contact people who are in a position to provide information about job leads and the hiring process at their company and to put you in touch with those who have the power to hire you. Give them a copy of your resume so they can speak knowledgeably about your skills and accomplishments. Who are these people? They can be

- *Friends, friends of your parents, neighbors, and relatives.* They know you and are the most likely prospects to offer to go out of their way to help you.
- *People you know through social, school, athletic, or community organizations.* If they aren't in a position to put you in touch with a job contact, they may know someone who can.
- *Alumni.* At many colleges and universities, the placement or alumni office tries to link up job hunting alumni with employers or alumni who are willing to offer their advice about how to get a job in their field.

Be sure to follow up on every suggestion. Get the spelling of every person's name, his or her job title, company, and phone number. Write down how your contact knows the person suggested and ask if it's all right for you to use his or her name. If you're not sure how the person suggested might be helpful to you in your job search, ask your contact for more information. It's almost always best to call rather than write. (If you can get the person on the line, you'll get immediate feedback.) After you talk, follow up with a thank-you letter and a copy of your resume. If you've arranged to see the person, take copies of your resume with you.

Beyond Networking

Using the telephone and library to target employers is a task many job hunters prefer to skip because it's time consuming and can be tedious or because they don't know their way around a library. But every hour you invest in locating and learning about potential employers will increase your chances for an interview and your chances to be hired. Your goal should be to develop a list of dozens of employers who hire people with your skills and experience. You can start your research at home with the *Yellow Pages*. Headings in it are straightforward—"Banks," "Lawyers," "Restaurants." If you're looking for a job in a field that doesn't directly service consumers (i.e., machine tooling), check the business-to-business section. In large cities, this may be a separate directory. Copy down the name, address, and telephone number of prospective employers.

Your next step is a trip to the business section of the local library. Don't be intimidated if you haven't used it before. You'll find most librarians eager to assist you. To add to your list of prospective employers, ask for the following reference books.

- *Standard & Poor's Register of Corporations, Directors and Executives,* published by McGraw-Hill (volume 2 lists companies by location).
- *The National Directory of Addresses and Phone Numbers,* published by Gale Research Inc.
- *Million Dollar Directory,* published by Dun & Bradstreet (volume 3 lists businesses geographically).
- *Job Seeker's Guide to Private and Public Companies,* published by Gale Research Inc.
- *Job Opportunities for Business and Liberal Arts Graduates,* published by Peterson's Guides, Inc.
- *Job Opportunities for Engineering, Science, and Computer Graduates,* published by Peterson's Guides, Inc.

If you know the industry you want to work in, you should also ask the librarian to recommend a specific reference book. If you want to work for a law firm, for example, *The Martindale-Hubbell Law Directory* would be a good starting point.

Your next task is to identify the manager in each company or organization on your list who heads up the division or department you hope to work in. Some reference books provide this information, but because people often change positions, your best bet is a phone call to the company switchboard. Ask the operator for the exact spelling of the person's name and his or her job title. To keep your phone costs down, get an 800 directory (i.e., the business edition of the *AT&T Toll-Free Directory*).

The more you understand about the current business situation of the employer you'll be talking to, the easier it will be to know how to talk about what you can do for that company. Articles that have been written within the last year about the industry or the employer are often the best sources of information and are easy to locate.

If you subscribe to a database information service such as CompuServe, DIALOG, or Prodigy, you can search for article citations and summaries on your computer. A less expensive alternative is to visit your local library. You may be able to use its computer or CD-ROM disks to do similar searches, or you can use standard reference books such as the *Business Periodicals Index,* the *New York Times Index,* or the *Wall Street Journal Index.*

If the prospective employer is a publicly traded company, call and request a copy of its annual report from its public relations or corporate communications department. Annual reports often describe organization structures and provide photos of office and plant facilities.

Now you can begin writing cover letters.

The Secrets of a Successful Cover Letter

Sending a resume without an accompanying letter is like giving a gift with no card—it's incomplete and can be confusing. You stand a much better chance of being invited for an interview if you take the trouble to briefly explain why you are writing to a particular employer. If you find the prospect of writing a cover letter intimidating, the following suggestions can make the process simpler.

Write to a specific person. It's far better to target someone at the department you'd like to work in who has the power to hire than it is to send your letter to someone in personnel. A manager receives far fewer resumes and is more likely to at least skim yours even if he or she isn't currently hiring. Even if it ends up getting passed on to personnel, it may get more attention (particularly if the manager attaches a positive comment) than one that was sent directly to personnel.

Explain your interest. In the first paragraph, mention how you heard about the job opening or why you are interested in applying for a job with the company. Try to be as specific as you can—say that you saw the company's ad, that a mutual friend recommended you contact the person, that an employee told you about plans for expansion. Be sure to get permission to name the people you refer to. If possible, discuss why the work of the department or company is of particular interest to you.

Avoid using phrases that sound canned or disingenuous, such as "your xyz department is the best one in the industry" or "working for a company such as yours, with its excellent reputation." Instead, attempt to relate your interests to the products or services of the employer: "Having been an amateur astronomer since high school, I would welcome the opportunity to use my promotional skills in the public relations department of the planetarium."

Describe your credentials. Don't lift parts of your resume and insert them into the cover letter. Instead, decide which skills, accomplishments, or experiences are particularly relevant to what the employer is looking for and describe them, incorporating terminology the employer has used in a help-wanted ad, written job description, or conversation, if possible. It's a good idea to refer back to your fact sheets or to the working draft of your resume to get ideas on language or details worth incorporating.

If, for example, the employer is a computer-hardware manufacturer looking for a technical writer, you might say, "Although I majored in English, I have completed a one-semester technical writing certificate program. I also received on-the-job training in an intensive one-month internship with Apple Computer Company." Mentioning two or three key credentials is plenty; after all, the purpose of the cover letter is to pique the interest of the employer.

State what you can do for the company. The purpose of the third paragraph is to set you apart as an applicant who understands the employer's needs, not as someone who is simply looking to better his or her own situation. You might write, "I'm confident that I can use my writing and presentation skills to increase attendance at the planetarium and would be prepared to share my ideas on how that might be done in an interview" or "I would enjoy the opportunity to put my selling skills to work for a company whose product line I'm already familiar with because of my experience."

Ask for an interview. If you haven't already mentioned that you would like a chance to meet in person, as was the case in the planetarium example, add a sentence that requests an interview. You might also indicate when it's easiest to reach you, whether it's all right for the employer to contact you at work, and when you'll be following up with a check-in phone call.

How to Respond to a Request for Salary Information

If you have been working in the field in which you plan to get a job, don't reveal salary information. It's to your advantage in a salary negotiation to have the employer tell you the range first. If the employer or help-wanted ad to which you are replying specifically requests such information, you're better off saying that you're looking for a salary that's in the going-rate range for someone with your experience. (In a recent survey conducted by Fox-Morris Associates, a Philadelphia-based executive search and outplacement consulting firm, almost 80 percent of human resource executives reported that they would call an applicant whose resume interested them, even if the person was outside an advertisement's salary guidelines.)

How to Give Your Cover Letter a Professional Look

Be sure that the design and look of your cover letter are as professional and inviting as your resume. You can achieve this if you do the following.

- Use the same type and size of paper as you did for your resume. Personal stationery, paper with the letterhead of your current (or past) employer, or plain typing paper are taboo.

- Use the same typeface as you did on your resume. For a long cover letter, a 10-point typeface will look best. For a short letter, a 12-point typeface is fine.
- Set up the letter using traditional business-letter techniques. The preferred format is to align your address, the date, the closing, and your name and phone number at the center of the page. The employer's name, address, and the salutation should be flush left.

Don't forget to proofread your letter and, if you are composing it on a computer, use the spell checking feature.

Sample Cover Letter

26 W. 75th Street
New York, NY 10023

June 1, 1991

Mrs. Ellen Goodrill, President
College Media Relations
411 Broad Street
Keene, NH 03413

Dear Ms. Goodrill:

We met briefly last winter when you visited my boss, Helen Sterling, director of Syracuse University's media relations department. One of my projects as an intern in that office was putting together a report documenting local print, radio, and TV stories on the AIDS research being done at the University's microbiology department. I was very impressed with the level of national coverage you later coordinated on the lab's work.

I recently graduated and am looking for a job with a public relations firm serving higher education clients. I feel I could be an asset to your firm. Why? Having written twenty-five stories for the campus newspaper, I understand how to position and develop a story idea. I am comfortable using research databases such as NEXIS and DIALOG. And as a customer service representative (summers during college), I developed an engaging phone manner and an ability to deal with all types of people. Of course, I'm willing to take on any responsibilities that come with an entry-level position with your firm.

I plan to be in the Keene area the week of July 1. Would it be possible to set up an appointment? I will call you next week.

Sincerely,

Judd Chasen
(212) 555-8070

A Final Word

I hope that you feel confident and optimistic about starting your job search as a result of reading *The 90-Minute Resume* and working through the process. Keep in mind that finding the right job may take weeks or months of looking. If you are not successful in getting interviews, you may have to become more aggressive in tracking down leads by talking to as many connected people as you can about what you are looking for. Or you may have to expand your geographic or career boundaries. Don't get discouraged if you get rejection after rejection. You need only one "yes" to get a job. And the more "no's" you hear, the better the odds are that it won't be long before you get that "yes."

I'm honored that you took my resume-writing advice to heart, and I promise you this: If you put the same level of concentrated energy into conducting your job search, the job you land will be rewarding.

Resume Makeovers

The sample resumes that appear in this section have been adapted from real resumes. Each is depicted before and after the job hunter went through the 90-minute process. Analyses of the biggest faults of the "before" version and of the strong points of the "after" version are provided.

The Chronological Format

The first two resumes presented in this section use the chronological format. This format should be your choice unless you have had extensive work experience through participation in a co-op program, internship, or part-time job that you feel would be more effectively presented as a set of skills in a functional or combination chronological/ functional format.

Resume 1

Nancy Baxter majored in genetics in college and wants to work full-time as a research assistant at a laboratory before continuing her graduate studies.

ANALYSIS

Even though Nancy's work experience is impressive, she should start off with her Education section because she is a recent graduate. Although her job descriptions imply she held a lot of responsibility, she hasn't provided the details that make it clear that that was the case. Overall, this "before" resume is too skeletal.

The numbers and descriptions Nancy added beneath her work descriptions and to her level of involvement in an important activity make her resume a standout. The streamlined design is more professional looking. (Typeface: Helvetica)

Before

Nancy Baxter
305 Channing Way
Berkeley, CA 94704
(415) 555-0985

WORK EXPERIENCE

<u>Laboratory Assistant</u>, Genetics Laboratory, University
of California at Berkeley, 1990-92 (fifteen hours a
week during school term)
— Prepared media and solutions, which involved use
  of pH meter
— Cared for lab animals
— Conducted supply and chemical inventories

<u>Assistant Laboratory Manager</u>, JDL Laboratories,
Summers 1990-91
— Researched new lab equipment
— Managed office staff of three
— Helped plan schedules for research work projects

<u>Tennis Instructor</u>, Claremont Racquet Club, Summers
1988-89

EDUCATION

B.S., Genetics, University of California, Berkeley,
1991, Magna Cum Laude

ACTIVITIES

<u>Coordinator, Speakers' Forum</u>, Student Genetics
Association, 1990
— Researched and contacted prominent scientists to
  participate in panel discussions

INTERESTS

Tennis and photography

After

Nancy Baxter
305 Channing Way
Berkeley, California 94704
(415) 635-0985

EDUCATION
B.S., Genetics, University of California at Berkeley, 1991, Magna Cum Laude

LABORATORY WORK EXPERIENCE

1990–92 (part-time)
Laboratory Assistant, Genetics Laboratory, University of California at Berkeley
- Selected for fellowship on basis of grade point average and "potential for success in science"
- Prepared media and solutions, which involved use of pH meter
- Cared for over 200 laboratory animals, including mice, rats, and rabbits
- Conducted supply and chemical inventories

Summers 1990–91
Assistant Laboratory Manager, JDL Laboratories
- Researched new lab equipment totaling $50,000, which was subsequently approved and purchased
- Managed office staff of three; developed new performance evaluation system, which was adopted
- Helped plan schedules for research work projects

ADDITIONAL WORK EXPERIENCE

Summers 1988–89
Tennis Instructor, Claremont Racquet Club

ACTIVITIES
Coordinator, Speakers' Forum, Student Genetics Association, 1991
- Researched and contacted prominent scientists to participate in five panel discussions on "hot" scientific issues; two events covered by local media

INTERESTS
Tennis (captain of women's collegiate team) and photography (have won two prizes in amateur competitions)

Resume 2

Jonathon, a recent college graduate, would like to use his graphic design skills in the art department of a magazine.

ANALYSIS

There is plenty of white space in Jonathon's "before" resume, which is a delight for any graphic designer, but there are woefully few details. The objective is long and rambling, and the personal information at the bottom of the resume is extraneous.

By talking about what he achieved in his only paid design job in this "after" resume, Jonathon makes a much stronger case for his candidacy. He has also added important details, such as earning most of his college expenses. While there is less white space, the picture of Jonathon as a talented and hard-working graphic designer is much more complete. (Typeface: Optima)

Before

Resume of   2 West Ridge Road
Jonathon Schuller   Greenwich, CT 06812
                                                    (203) 555-0063

OBJECTIVE: I would like to work for and become an
                asset to a magazine publication in their
                design and production department and
                eventually assume responsibility as an
                Art Director and contribute to the
                overall appearance of a publication

EMPLOYMENT: ART DIRECTOR
                10/89-present
                Bowling Green State University Alumni
                 Association
                Bowling Green, Ohio 43502

                CREW FOREMAN
                Summers, 1989-91
                Johnson Pools
                Stamford, CT 06817

SKILLS: PageMaker 4.01, Aldus SuperPaint 3.0,
                Aldus FreeHand 3.0, Quark XPress 3.0,
                Microsoft Word 4.0

EDUCATION: BOWLING GREEN STATE UNIVERSITY
                1988-1992
                DEGREE: B.F.A.
                GRADUATION: June 1992
                MAJOR: GRAPHIC DESIGN

ACTIVITIES: Member, Desktop Designers SIG, CompuServe
                Member, National Association of Desktop
                 Publishers

INTERESTS: Reading magazines, karate

PERSONAL: Born: October 1, 1970, New York, NY
                Marital Status: Single
                Health: Excellent
                Willing to travel and relocate

After

Jonathon Schuller
2 West Ridge Road
Greenwich, CT 06812
(203) 555-0063

OBJECTIVE:

An entry-level position in the art department of a magazine

EDUCATION:

B.F.A., June 1992, Bowling Green State University
Bowling Green, Ohio
- Earned 80 percent of college expenses through summer and part-time jobs

GRAPHIC DESIGN
EXPERIENCE:

Art Director, Bowling Green State University
Alumni Association, 10/89–present
- Created alumni association logo that won first place in student graphic design competition that was basis for landing job
- Designed fifty-page magazine, "How to Start a Local Chapter," and produced it for 25 percent less than what was budgeted by using desktop publishing program
- Developed prototype for four-color monthly alumni magazine; produced fifteen issues, one of which won an award from the Student Association of Graphic Designers for innovative design

SUMMER WORK
EXPERIENCE:

Crew Foreman, Johnson Pools, Stamford, Connecticut, Summers 1989–91
- Coordinated crew of five
- Installed fifty in-ground pools; received numerous letters from satisfied customers

SKILLS:

PageMaker 4.01, Aldus SuperPaint 3.0, Aldus FreeHand 3.0, Quark XPress 3.0, Microsoft Word 4.0

ACTIVITIES:

Member, Desktop Designers SIG, CompuServe
Member, National Association of Desktop Publishers

INTERESTS:

Studying and critiquing magazine design, karate (have earned brown belt)

The Functional Format

You've already done most of the work needed to create a functional resume. You identified the main areas of expertise required by your job target in "First, Your Fact Sheets," and, in "What Are You an Expert At?," you grouped descriptions of tasks and accomplishments from each job or activity related to your target under the appropriate area of expertise. So pull out those work sheets and let's move ahead!

With this format, it's best to use the past tense of all action verbs, even for descriptions of current tasks. After each entry, list the year or years you performed or accomplished it so that the resume reader can quickly determine when you acquired the skill. Next, create a job history section. List your job title, the name of the employer, location (if necessary), and the dates of employment.

EXAMPLE

Indiana University, Bloomington, Indiana, 1984–present

> College Adviser, 1992–present
>
> Program Assistant, Arts and Sciences Division, 1991–92
>
> Teaching Assistant, English Department, 1/90–12/90

These two sections—areas of expertise (there should be two to four of them) and work history—are the heart of a functional resume. Follow the directions in "Create a Working Draft" on page 49 for the remaining sections. The sequence should be:

- Identification
- Job Objective or Summary of Qualifications (both optional)
- Areas of Expertise
- Work History

- Skills (optional)
- Education
- Interests

Resume 3

Jason is a 1992 graduate who hopes to parlay his fund-raising and coordination skills into a job with a lobbying organization.

ANALYSIS

In Jason's "before" resume, the Identification section has too many bullets and uses a disproportionately large point size. It doesn't appear that Jason has given careful thought to the organization of his resume, and he hasn't provided numbers to back up his accomplishments or provided a context for his responsibilities.

In his "after" resume, Jason has made it much easier for a potential employer to see why he has something to offer. Because he developed the skills needed for lobbying and fund-raising working in a gubernatorial campaign and through his university activities, Jason was able to use a functional format to his advantage. This version is much more design oriented and is easy to read. (Typeface: Bookman)

Before

• Jason Snyder • 38-49 Crescent Street • Bay Village, Ohio • 44039 • (216) 662-9854 (as of 6/15/92) •

EDUCATION

Bachelor of Arts, Speech Communication, Case Western
Reserve University, 1992, Cum Laude

ACTIVITIES

Volunteer staff worker, Ohio Gubernatorial
Fund-Raising, 1988-90
— Worked on a part-time basis making phone calls,
  asking for campaign donations, helping out with
  mailings, and making arrangements for candidate
  to visit Ohio colleges

President, Student Activities Board, 1991-92
— Oversaw budget of $300,000, set up new mailing
  system to students, approved and scheduled
  forty-five campus events

Student Coordinator, Cuyahoga, Ohio, Health Fair,
Summer 1987
— Helped raise money and material from local
  businesses
— Found volunteers to help man booths

Student Volunteer—Helped raise money for university
in telethons

WORK EXPERIENCE

Bartender, The Rusty Scupper, Summers 1988-91
— Served drinks, assisted food-and-beverage
  manager with purchase orders, trained new
  bartenders

INTERESTS

Hiking and electoral politics

After

Jason Snyder

38–49 Crescent Street
Bay Village, Ohio 44039

Phone: (216) 662-9854
(as of 6/16/92)

**JOB
OBJECTIVE**
A position as a research assistant or grassroots fund-raiser with an advocacy group

EDUCATION
Bachelor of Arts, Speech Communication, Case Western Reserve University, 1992, Cum Laude

CAPABILITIES

Fund Raising
- Helped raise funds in successful Ohio 1990 gubernatorial campaign, 1988–90
- Solicited printed materials and $5,000 in donations from corporate sponsors of health fair, 1987
- Participated in five telethons sponsored by university alumni office; personally raised $15,000 in pledges, 1988–92

Administration
- Planned various candidate appearances, including locations and facilities; organized schedule of events, 1988–90
- Implemented database mailing systems, 1991–92
- Authorized expenditure of $300,000 budget, 1991–92

Management
- Mobilized volunteers and coordinated their work at conference, 1987
- Devised system for collection, organization, and dissemination of information to student body of 35,000, 1991–92

WORK EXPERIENCE

Volunteer Staff Worker, Ohio Gubernatorial Fund Raising, 1988–1990
President, Student Activities Board, Case Western Reserve University, 1991–92
Coordinator, Cuyahoga, Ohio, Health Fair, Summer, 1987
Bartender, The Rusty Scupper, Summers 1988–1991

INTERESTS

Hiking the Appalachian Trail, speaking to grade school students about electoral politics

Resume 4

Jacqueline has worked full-time since graduating from high school and earned an associate degree in marketing on a part-time basis. She hopes to move up to a marketing job with a financial services company, the same kind of employer she has been working for as a telemarketer.

ANALYSIS

While it is apparent that Jacqueline has been steadily employed and has been promoted, her "before" resume doesn't provide the punch necessary to make it a great marketing tool. The Identification section is unsophisticated and the design is lackluster.

The functional format works well for Jacqueline, who wants to emphasize the role her work experience has played in preparing her for a marketing position. She has also strengthened her "after" resume by adding details and numbers about her responsibilities and accomplishments. Finally, the design is easy to read and professional looking. (Typeface: Times)

Before

Introducing

Jacqueline Lionel
70 Maple Drive
Fairfield, Connecticut

(203) 555-2389 (home)   (203) 555-7900 (work)

Education

A.A., Accounting, Bridgeport Community College, August
1992
High School Diploma,. Holy Cross High School, June 1986

Job History

Salesnet, a division of Dun & Bradstreet, Norwalk,
Connecticut
Telemarketing Supervisor, 12/90-present

Responsible for training, supervising, and scripting
of client calls
Telemarketing Communicator, 10/88-12/90

Sold equity access accounts, telephone services,
encyclopedias, and children's books; demonstrated
telemarketing for major clients; developed scripting of
calls.

Luv Baby Foods, Stamford, Connecticut
Customer Service Representative, 7/86-9/88

Answered customer questions about company products

Interests

Hang gliding, listening to classical music

After

Jacqueline Lionel
70 Maple Drive
Fairfield, Connecticut

(203) 555-2389 (home)   (203) 555-7900 (work)

Qualifications Six years of telemarketing and customer service
Summary   experience, coupled with a degree in marketing and a
                   solid understanding of financial services products

Capabilities

Marketing/   • Developed new scripts which resulted in a 20 percent
Sales   increase in sale of equity access accounts
10/88–12/90   • Sold telephone services, encyclopedias, and children's
                   books
                 • Recognized as salesperson of month four times

Supervision/ • Coordinated efforts of ten telemarketers and office staff
Training   of two
12/90–present   • Recruited five new hires and trained them in
                   telemarketing techniques

Customer   • Credited by company president with preventing a costly
Service   lawsuit because of my handling of an irate customer
7/86–9/88   • Answered average of twenty-five calls a day

Work History **Salesnet,** a division of Dun & Bradstreet,
                 Telemarketing Supervisor, 12/90–present
                 Telemarketing Communicator, 10/88–12/90

                 Luv Baby Foods, Stamford, Connecticut
                 Customer Service Representative, 7/86–9/88

Education   A.A., Marketing, Bridgeport Community College,
                   January 1992
                 High school diploma, Holy Cross High School,
                   June 1986

Interests   Hang gliding, listening to classical music

The Combination Chronological/ Functional Format

The last resume presented in this section uses a combination chronological/functional format. In addition to presenting your experience in an easy-to-read manner, it allows you to highlight the functional skills you have gained as a result of that experience.

Resume 5

Eliza has worked for a manufacturer and a retailer part-time and during summers. Now that she has an associate degree in fashion merchandising, she'd like to make the leap to clothing buyer.

ANALYSIS

Eliza's "before" resume is serviceable but not stellar, even though her experience is very strong. She can do a better job analyzing her accomplishments and responsibilities and positioning herself for her targeted job.

After looking at the job responsibilities involved in her job target, Eliza was able to group her job tasks into those areas in this "after" resume. She decided a chronological format would best highlight her promotions and the breadth of her job experience. By combining it with a functional format and putting the area of expertise next to the job tasks, however, she makes it easy for a potential employer to see why she is qualified to be a clothing buyer. (Typeface: Optima)

Before

Eliza Wong
700 N. Altamont Way, Montclair, NJ 09087   (201) 555-7890 (home)

Education: A.A., 1992, Fashion Merchandising,
            Bergen County Community College
            Graduated 1990, Livingston High School

Work
Experience: *Floater, Ellen Tracy, Summers 1990, 1991*

- oversaw shipments of clothing to adjunct warehouse, including quality-control inspections and storage
- assisted in supervision of inspectors
- made decisions on which clothing flaws warranted garment being sent to factory store

Floor Assistant, Bloomingdales, Hackensack, NJ, Summers 1988, 1989

- monitored flow of sales clerks to ensure all stations covered
- helped designers to come up with department themes and seasonal displays
- made recommendations to buyers based on observations of inventory and customer buying habits

Sales Clerk, Bloomingdales, Hackensack, NJ, 1986-88, part-time

- developed experience in women's, children's, and men's fashion areas
- responsible for accurate financial transactions with customers

Interests: Sewing, hiking, singing

After

Eliza Wong

700 N. Altamont Way • Montclair, NJ 09087 • (201) 555-7890 (home)

Objective: A position as a clothing or accessories buyer

Education: A.A., 1992, Fashion Merchandising, Bergen County
Community College
Graduated 1990, Livingston High School

**Work
Experience:**   Floater, Ellen Tracy, Summers 1990, 1991

Supervision   • Oversaw shipments of clothing worth up to $50,000 to
adjunct warehouse
• Assisted in supervision of quality-control inspectors

Quality   • Conducted inspections of clothing for flaws and damage
Control   • Decided which clothing flaws warranted garment being
sent to factory store

Floor Assistant, Bloomingdales, Hackensack, NJ,
Summers 1988, 1989

Supervision   • Monitored sales clerk check-ins to ensure coverage

Merchandising   • Worked with designers to come up with department
themes and seasonal displays
• Made recommendations to buyers based on observations
of inventory and customer buying habits

Sales Clerk, Bloomingdales, Hackensack, NJ, 1986–88,
part-time

Merchandising   • Developed sense of consumer buying habits and
preferences by talking with customers in women's,
children's, and men's fashion areas

Sales   • Got involved in customer decision making by helping to
accessorize and style look

Interests: Sewing (have created my own designs and sold over 100
items), hiking in the Adirondacks, singing in local choir

We'd Like to Hear from You

If *The 90-Minute Resume* has helped you, you can help us. The best way to ensure that the 90-minute process continues to work is to hear the comments and suggestions of those who have put it to use.

- What features were most helpful in creating your resume?

- Did you receive comments from employers, agencies, or others about your resume?

- Is there anything in particular about the 90-minute process that you feel could be improved?

- Do you have suggestions for what you'd like to see added or changed in a future edition?

- Would you find a computerized version of *The 90-Minute Resume* helpful? If yes, please indicate the type of personal computer you would use.

"Before" and "after" versions of your resume will also be helpful for future editions of the book. Please send your correspondence to: Peggy Schmidt, *The 90-Minute Resume*, c/o Peterson's Guides, Inc., P.O. Box 2123, Princeton, NJ 08543-2123.

About the Author

Peggy Schmidt writes "Your New Job," a nationally syndicated weekly newspaper column, and is the author of *The 90-Minute Resume*, for job hunters who are writing their resume for the first time, and *Making It on Your First Job*. She has also been a career columnist for *Glamour* and *New Woman* magazines. As career coordinator for the New York University Summer Publishing Institute, Schmidt has given resume tips and job hunting advice to hundreds of individuals.